SCIENCE WORKS!

SOUND

STEVE PARKER

For a free color catalog describing Gareth Stevens Publishing's list of high-quality books and multimedia programs, call 1-800-542-2595 (USA) or 1-800-461-9120 (Canada). Gareth Stevens Publishing's Fax: (414) 225-0377.
See our catalog, too, on the World Wide Web: http://gsinc.com

Library of Congress Cataloging-in-Publication Data

Parker, Steve.
    Sound / by Steve Parker.
      p. cm. -- (Science works!)
    Includes index.
    Summary: Uses brief text, illustrations, quizzes, games, and experiments to explain all about sound, which sounds animals and humans can hear, how sound can smash matter, and how it can heal.
    ISBN 0-8368-1965-9 (lib. bdg.)
    1. Sound -- Juvenile literature. 2. Sound--Experiments--Juvenile literature. [1. Sound. 2. Sound--Experiments. 3. Experiments.]
    I. Title. II. Series: Parker, Steve. Science Works!
QC225.5.P37 1997
534--dc21   97-11525

First published in North America in 1997 by
Gareth Stevens Publishing
1555 North RiverCenter Drive, Suite 201
Milwaukee, WI 53212 USA

This U.S. edition © 1997 by Gareth Stevens, Inc. Created with original © 1995 by Macdonald Young Books Ltd., Campus 400, Maylands Avenue, Hemel Hempstead, Hertfordshire, England HP2 7EZ. Additional end matter © 1997 by Gareth Stevens, Inc.

Illustrators: Maltings Partnership, Chris Lyons, Martin Woodward, Stephen Mclean, Treve Tamblin. Picture credits: Sally & Richard Greenhill, 35; The Kobal Collection, 38; Redferns, 4, 21, 33, 44; Rex Features, 29; Zefa, 6, 9, 10, 13, 14, 17, 36, 40, 42, 45.

Printed in Mexico

1 2 3 4 5 6 7 8 9 01 00 99 98 97

SCIENCE WORKS!

SOUND

STEVE PARKER

Gareth Stevens Publishing
MILWAUKEE

20.00

CONTENTS

Words that appear in the glossary are in **boldface** type the first time they occur in the text.

SOUND

Our ears let us hear millions of sounds during our lives, but something we never hear is the sound of silence. The world is a noisy place — from wind and rain to the sounds that people and many types of animals use to communicate to the breathing and heartbeats of our own bodies. In our modern world, the science of sound — **acoustics** — has hundreds of uses. It is applied to the design of house walls and concert halls, to the recording of speech and music, and to noise pollution in cities. Sounds bring us information, pleasure, and sometimes even pain. They play a central part in daily life.

The story of sound

This book contains ideas about sound, and the way we make and use sounds — from the echoing caves of Stone Age times to the modern world of radio, television, compact discs, and electronic digital sampling.

The first section of this book examines the nature of sound. What is it? How does it get from one place to another? What are **pitch**, **frequency**, and loudness?

The second section looks at sounds in nature — from the whisper of the wind in grass to the menacing rumble of thunder to the many animals that use sound to hunt, repel rivals, frighten enemies, attract mates, and care for babies.

The third section describes the numerous devices that produce sounds, and how they work. Examples are the voice box in the human body, musical instruments, loudspeakers, and the sonic boom of faster-than-sound aircraft.

The fourth section shows how sounds are detected in a variety of ways, including with the ears and with microphones found in telephones and many other pieces of equipment.

The fifth section describes how inventors and scientists have recorded sounds in different ways, from the wavy groove in a vinyl recording to microscopic pits on a compact disc, and how these sounds are played back again.

The last section looks at some unusual sounds, such as the warning wail of an emergency siren. It also examines how our world seems to be getting steadily noisier.

FAMOUS FIRSTS

Knowledge thrives on firsts, such as the first person to discover a scientific law or make an invention. The *Famous Firsts* panels describe these first achievers.

DIY SCIENCE

Follow in the footsteps of well-known scientists by trying the tests and experiments in "Do-It-Yourself" form, using everyday materials, as shown in the *DIY Science* panels.

SPECIAL FX

Scientific processes and principles can have fascinating, even startling, results. The *Special FX* projects show you how to produce these special effects. Most items are readily available in your home.

WHAT IS SOUND?

We cannot see or feel sound. But our ears tell us that sound is all around. What exactly is a sound, and why is it invisible? How does it move, and why does it fade away? Scientific research, dating from experiments in the seventeenth century, has given us most of the answers to the ancient mysteries of sound.

FAMOUS FIRSTS

Robert Boyle's (1627-1691) experiments with the air pump led to his discovery of the link between a gas's pressure, volume, and temperature — known as Boyle's law.

SOUND AND THE AIR PUMP

In the 1640s, German physicist and engineer Otto von Guericke (1602-1686) modified the water pump into an air pump. The air pump could remove most of the air from a container, leaving almost nothing — a partial vacuum. When a ringing bell was put in the container and the air removed, the bell's sound faded away. This was the first evidence that sound needed something to travel through. English scientists Robert Boyle, Robert Hooke, and Francis Hauksbee made better pumps. In 1705, Hauksbee put a clock in a jar and removed the air, and the clock's ticks went silent.

In ancient times, people commonly believed that gods made the huge, frightening sounds of natural events, such as thunderstorms, volcanic eruptions, and earthquakes. But early scientists wanted to find out more.

Around 2,530 years ago, the Greek mathematician Pythagoras observed musical instruments. He saw that when strings of different lengths vibrate, or shake rapidly back and forth, the shorter strings produce higher sounds. Two centuries later, Aristotle suggested that sound traveled due to some motion or movement in the air.

During the Dark Ages in Europe, there was little progress in science. Progress came in the seventeenth century, including the invention of the vacuum — a place that contains nothing, not even air.

Further experiments led to the idea that sound travels in waves. These are usually drawn as a wavy line, like ripples on a pond.

More than 2,350 years ago, the great Greek thinker and naturalist Aristotle pondered on many problems, including the nature of sound. He believed correctly that it had something to do with invisible movements in air.

In ancient Greece, builders planned performance places, called amphitheaters, with bowl-like shapes and rising rows or tiers of seats. This design prevented sounds from being blown away by the wind. It also allowed the audience to be near the stage, so people could see and hear clearly.

DIY SCIENCE

SEEING SOUNDS

Everything in the Universe is made up of tiny particles called **atoms** either on their own or joined to other atoms to form **molecules**. Individual atoms and molecules are far too small to see. But when millions of them are lumped together, they become visible. This happens in solids where the molecules are close together. They are held in position and hardly move. In liquids, the molecules are farther apart and can move more easily. In gases, they are spaced even farther apart, and they are invisible. Air is a mixture of gas molecules, mainly those of nitrogen and oxygen, with smaller amounts of the rarer atmospheric gases such as argon and carbon dioxide. Sound waves consist of coordinated movements or vibrations of these air molecules. They are in the form of waves of higher and lower air pressure that are released from the sound source. When these waves arrive at a thin, flexible sheet or membrane, they cause the sheet to shake or vibrate with visible results.

You need

Plastic bowl, cookie sheet, plastic wrap, large rubber band, wooden spoon, salt or sugar, tape, scissors.

1. Place the plastic wrap over the bowl, and pull it to remove creases. Carefully cut the plastic wrap, making it about 2 inches (5 centimeters) larger than the bowl.

2. Pull the plastic tightly and evenly over the bowl. Secure it with the rubber band so it is taut like a drum head.

3. Secure the edge of the plastic firmly to the bowl with tape placed at regular intervals.

4. Place some grains of salt or sugar on the plastic. Hold the cookie sheet nearby, and strike it with the wooden spoon. Do you *see* the sounds in the salt or sugar?

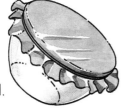

FASCINATING FACTS

Sounds bounce and echo in a circle around the Whispering Gallery of St. Paul's Cathedral, London.

- In the Greek myths, Echo, a nymph, kept the goddess Hera talking while Hera's husband Zeus spent time with other women. Hera found out and put a curse on Echo. The nymph could now only repeat what others had said.

Striking the cookie sheet produces sound waves in the air.

The sound waves make the thin plastic wrap vibrate and the grains of salt or sugar "dance."

9

Peak

Amplitude

Trough

Displacement

One wavelength

Any sound, from a whisper to the deafening roar of a jet engine, can be represented as a wavy line called a sound wave, as shown above.

The idea of waves is useful for describing features of sound, such as **wavelength** and frequency. Wavelength is the distance between two similar points of successive waves. Frequency is the number of vibrations per second. It is related to a sound's pitch. Short wavelength and high frequency mean a high pitch, such as a squeak. Long wavelength and low frequency mean a low or deep pitch, such as a rumble.

In reality, sound exists as the vibrations or movements of molecules. In air, the molecules are those of the various gases in the mixture, such as nitrogen and oxygen. A sound is the vibration of molecules in a certain way — a lot, then a little, than a lot again, and so on. As the molecules vibrate, they can be squeezed closer together (compressed), or spaced farther apart (expanded).

Gas molecules floating in air collide with each other and bounce away in the same way that fast-moving marbles on a table rebound off each other.

FAMOUS FIRSTS

FREQUENCY AND WAVELENGTH
A wavelength is the distance between a point on one wave, such as the peak, and the same point on the next wave. The distance is measured in feet or meters. The frequency is the number of complete waves that pass a place in a certain time, usually one second. It is the same as the number of waves, vibrations, or cycles per second. Frequency is measured in units called Hertz (Hz), named after German scientist Heinrich Hertz. The sound of the note middle C has a wavelength of 3.9 feet (1.2 meters) and a frequency of 256 Hertz. As the wavelength gets longer, the frequency gets lower and the sound is deeper in pitch. Shorter wavelengths mean higher frequencies and sounds that are shriller in pitch.

Heinrich Hertz (1857-1894)

SPECIAL FX

WHEN SOUNDS TRAVEL FASTER
Sound vibrations travel not only through air, but through other gases, liquids, and solids. In fact, sounds travel much faster and farther through most liquids and solids, compared to air *(see page 17)*. This includes the solid ground below our feet. If you put your ear to the ground, you may hear the drumming of an approaching vehicle or the thud of footsteps before these sounds reach you through the air. This is why expert trackers lie down and listen to the ground — to detect the thud of distant hooves or the rumble of faraway wheels.

The thunderous hooves of migrating wildebeest can be heard sooner and more clearly from several miles (kilometers) away by listening through the ground rather than the air.

SPECIAL FX

BOUNCING SOUNDS

When sound waves in air reach a solid, what happens next depends on the nature of the substance. If the substance is hard and smooth, like cardboard or a brick wall, the sounds bounce off in the same way that light rays bounce back from a mirror. We call this reflection. The reflected sound is known as an **echo**. If the solid substance is uneven and soft, like cotton, it absorbs much of the sound energy. So there is little or no reflection. This test shows that sounds reflect from a surface at the same angle at which they strike it.

You need
Piece of thick cardboard, sound source such as a ticking clock, two tubes of cardboard about 16 inches (40 cm) long and 2-4 inches (5-10 cm) wide.

1. Prop the cardboard up. Place a tube at an angle in front of it, as shown. Put the clock at the other end of the tube. Sound waves travel along the tube, hit the cardboard and reflect, or bounce off.

2. Put one end of the other tube near the cardboard to catch the echoes. Listen at the tube's other end and alter its angle until the echoes are loudest. This should be at an equal but opposite angle to the first tube. Repeat the test after altering the angle of the first tube, to check your results.

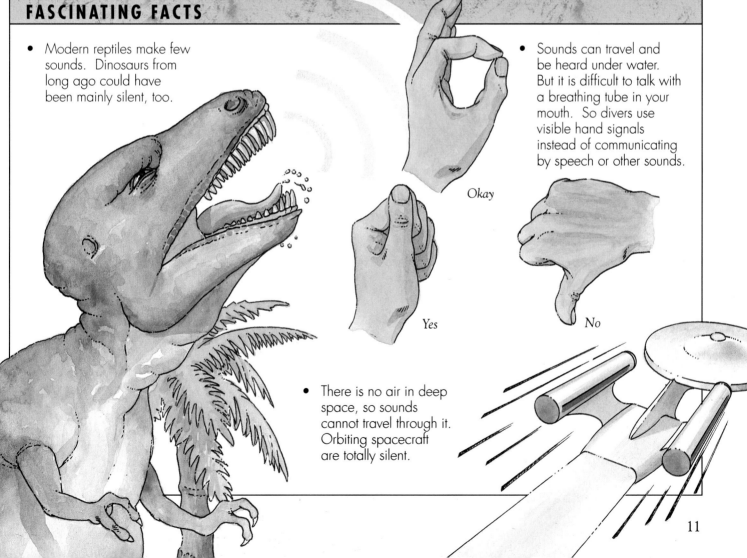

FASCINATING FACTS

• Modern reptiles make few sounds. Dinosaurs from long ago could have been mainly silent, too.

• Sounds can travel and be heard under water. But it is difficult to talk with a breathing tube in your mouth. So divers use visible hand signals instead of communicating by speech or other sounds.

Okay

Yes

No

• There is no air in deep space, so sounds cannot travel through it. Orbiting spacecraft are totally silent.

SOUND PRODUCED
[by voice box]
- Human   80-1,500 Hz
- Cat   750-1,500 Hz
- Robin   2,000-15,000 Hz
- Bat   10,000-150,000 Hz
- Dolphin   200-200,000 Hz

SOUND DETECTED
[by ears]
- Human   25-20,000 Hz
- Cat   60-60,000 Hz
- Robin   250-20,000 Hz
- Bat   1,000-200,000 Hz
- Dolphin   150-200,000 Hz

The sounds produced by different devices and animals vary widely across the frequency spectrum, from extremely low-pitched to incredibly high-pitched. We can only hear some of them because our ears detect a limited range of frequencies.

In air, these are regions of high and low air pressure. The regions pass outward from the sound source, like ripples on a pond. The water molecules in the pond's ripple bob up and down, but they do not move far. Air molecules do much the same when sound passes through the air. Even with an extremely loud sound, air molecules vibrate by only .00394 inch (0.1 millimeter).

We can hear some of the clicks and squeaks made by dolphins. They also make other sounds too high for humans to hear. But other dolphins can hear the sounds.

TRUMPETERS ON A TRAIN
Austrian physicist Christian Doppler (1803-1853) discovered the effect named after him in 1842 *(see below)*. At the time, there were few vehicles traveling fast enough for people to hear the Doppler effect. In 1845, a group of trumpet players rode in a railway carriage at high speed past listeners to demonstrate the effect.

The Doppler effect also happens with light from stars. If a star is moving away from us, its individual light pattern is moved or shifted toward the red end of the light spectrum. Astronomers use this "red shift" to calculate distances and speeds of stars.

THE DOPPLER EFFECT
Listen to a car the next time one speeds past. The sound from its engine seems to change from a higher to lower pitch. This is the Doppler effect. Any source producing sound and moving along moves a short distance between sending out each wave. So the waves traveling forward from it are squeezed closer together, while those behind are stretched farther apart. Closer waves mean a higher frequency or pitch, which you hear as the sound-maker approaches you. When it passes, you hear waves that are farther apart, with a lower frequency or pitch.

Sound waves farther apart [lower frequency and pitch].

Moving sound source

Sound waves closer together [higher frequency and pitch].

NEEEE-AAAA-OOOOW

The faster a sound source moves and the purer the sound it makes, the clearer you can hear the Doppler effect. The effect happens clearly with the engines in motorcycles, which run very fast with a high-pitched whine. But you can test the Doppler effect even at low speeds if you use a sound source with a pure and fairly high frequency, like a whistle.

You need
Friend with a bicycle, whistle, an open and safe place to cycle.

1. Stand or sit still in the middle of the space. Have your friend bicycle past you, speeding up as much as safely possible.

2. As your friend gets within about 30 feet (10 m) of you, have him or her blow the whistle and continue to blow while going past you, to about 30 feet (10 m) on the other side.

3. As your friend goes past, you should hear the whistle suddenly fall in pitch slightly, from higher to lower. This is the Doppler effect. Listen to the whistle while you are both still. Its pitch should remain somewhere in the middle.

- The Doppler effect is most noticeable when motorcycles or race cars pass by or when an emergency vehicle passes by blaring a siren.

- The Doppler effect applies to any type of wave, where the wave source is moving relative to the receiver. This includes sound and electromagnetic waves, such as radio waves, microwaves, visible light, and X rays.

- The speed-measuring radar devices used by police rely on the Doppler effect; so do some types of satellite navigation used by aircraft, ships, mapmakers, surveyors, and explorers.

Snow falls and settles in virtual silence. But when many tons of snow slide in an avalanche, it crackles, grates, and scrapes, and makes the ground tremble.

NATURAL SOUNDS

It is summer in the country. Birds sing, a cow chews its cud, and a slight breeze stirs the leaves. But wait. There is a peal of thunder. The birds squawk, and the cows grunt as the wind whips through the branches. Natural sounds have many sources and meanings.

Anywhere on Earth, you can hear the sounds of nature. The sounds come mainly from natural events, from the weather, and from living things. Natural events vary from the deafening roar of a volcanic eruption to a shuddering clap of thunder, from the pounding and sliding of a rockfall to the eerie crackling and grating of a snow avalanche, and from the thunderous booming of a waterfall to the sharp cracks and hisses of a brushfire. The weather gives us many familiar daily sounds that vary from comforting to alarming and can affect our moods and emotions. Wind blows gently or howls angrily. Rain patters lightly or splatters fiercely on window panes. Waves lap quietly on sandy beaches, then crash with ferocious power against the rocks. A trickling stream may swell into a raging torrent. All these sounds come from movements and vibrations of objects, which produce sound waves in the surrounding air.

There are also hundreds of natural voices — the sounds that creatures make as they go about their daily lives. Some are gentle and soothing to our ears, such as the cooing of pigeons and the purring of cats. Others are harsh

FAMOUS FIRSTS

The sound pulses reflect from objects, including the bat's prey.

A flying bat emits high-frequency sound pulses.

The bat hears sound echoes.

NAVIGATING BY SOUND
Bats find their way in the dark with their ears. A flying bat emits high-frequency squeaks and clicks, mostly too shrill for human ears, but not for the bat. The sounds bounce off close objects. The bat listens to the pattern of returning echoes in order to "see." The system is called **echolocation** and is a type of **sonar** (see page 43). It was first studied in bats by Donald Griffin in the late 1930s at Harvard University in Massachusetts. He was following earlier research by Italian scientist Lazarro Spallanzani (see opposite).

Sonagrams are diagrams of sounds, showing the frequency and timing of the sounds.

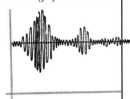

This one shows two of a bat's echolocation clicks.

DIY SCIENCE

THE DAWN CHORUS
At dawn, birds sing to tell each other who lives where, who is looking for a mate, and who is in charge of a territory. Note the calls of various birds, and write them in a nature diary. Does the dawn chorus begin at the same time each day, or is it linked to the time of sunrise? Do the various birds sing in the same order each morning?

SPECIAL FX

WIND WHISTLES AND HOWLS

How does the wind make so many different noises as it blows among trees or buildings? The moving air sets up vibrations as it goes through gaps or openings. These vibrations create sound waves. You can see this with a "wind tube." Hold one end of a tube, and twirl the other end around so that it passes through the air (rather than the air blowing past it) to give a wind effect.

You need

A tube of flexible plastic about 3 feet (1 m) long and 2-4 inches (5-10 cm) wide, paper funnel, plastic wrap, tape, scissors.

1. Twirl the tube so that air passes the moving end. Hear how it hums or howls, like wind blowing past a small opening. Does the speed of your twirling affect the pitch or loudness?

2. Enlarge the size of the opening of the twirling end by taping a funnel made from paper to it, as shown. Does this affect the pitch or loudness?

3. Make the opening smaller by covering the end with plastic wrap, with a small hole carefully cut in it. How does it sound now? What happens if you twirl the tube outside in the wind?

FASCINATING FACTS

- Lazarro Spallanzani was the first scientist to think that bats did not need their eyes to fly in the dark. In the 1790s, he tested pipistrelle bats in dark rooms to show they did not need sight to avoid obstacles. But if their ears were blocked, they flew less skillfully. He proposed that bats could "see" with their ears. People did not believe him until, over one hundred years later, scientists proved the theory using sound recordings, microphones, and loudspeakers.

Drum fish

- In the 1950s, American engineers set up underwater listening posts, using microphones to detect the sounds of enemy ships and submarines. The microphones picked up a deep humming noise with a constant frequency that could last more than thirty minutes. The engineers were sure the noise was made by the enemy, but it was the song of a finback whale.

- Many animals are named after the sounds they make, such as the drum fish, the bell-bird of Australia, and the spring peeper frog of North America.

Finback whale

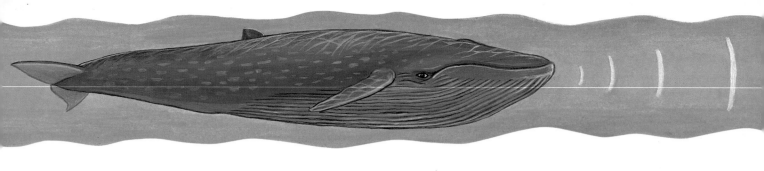

Many whales produce their songs about 66-82 feet (20-25 m) below the surface of the water. Sounds travel well in water at the temperature and pressure found there.

and scary, like a dog's snarl or a rabbit's squeal. Animals make these sounds for good reason. If we can learn the meanings of their songs and calls, we can understand more about nature.

The lowest sounds in the African bush are the rumblings of the elephant, too deep for human ears to hear. These sounds travel for several miles (kilometers). The loudest sounds in the tropical jungle are the whoops of the howler monkey from South America.

DIY SCIENCE

HOWL LIKE THE HOWLER!
The howler monkey makes an incredibly loud call by blowing air through its large voice box, making it vibrate strongly as a **resonating** chamber *(see pages 30 and 32).*

You need
Several plastic drink bottles, scissors.

1. Carefully cut one bottle in half, as shown. Place it near your mouth (not over the mouth) and "howl" loudly into it.

2. Alter the pitch and volume of your howl, until you hear the bottle "catch" the sound and make it louder, or amplify it. The bottle is acting like the howler monkey's large voice box — as a resonating chamber.

3. Cut other bottles to make chambers of various sizes. Which one resonates at the highest pitch?

FASCINATING FACTS

THE CRICKET COMB
Crickets chirp by rubbing a leg across a wing or vein. The leg has small "teeth" along its edge. These catch on the wing or vein and produce sound waves. You can mimic a cricket using a plastic comb.

You need
Large and small plastic hair combs; cardboard, plastic, and metal items to rub on the teeth.

FAMOUS FIRSTS

- Scientists continually make new discoveries in nature. For instance, they once thought that crocodiles were terrible parents, sometimes even eating their babies. Now we know that the mother crocodile does not eat her young but instead is carrying them to safety. When the babies are ready to hatch from their eggs on the riverbank, they squeak loudly. The mother helps them out of their shells. Then she carries them in her mouth to the water.

Eating their young would not be a good survival strategy for crocodiles. In fact, research shows that they have higher intelligence than lizards and snakes.

FASCINATING FACTS

Mynah

Macaw or parrot

- The loudest animal sounds are the deep grunts made by the world's largest animal, the blue whale. These grunts are estimated at 188 dB *(see pages 30-31)*, which would deafen a human. The grunts can be detected over a distance of almost 500 miles (800 km). Sounds travel more than four times faster in water than air — over 3,100 miles (5,000 km) per hour. In steel, sound travels more than three times faster than in water.

- Some birds can imitate or copy various sounds, including other birds and animals, human voices, and even machines and engines. The Australian lyrebird can mimic a tractor, a chainsaw, and a falling tree. Parrots and macaws are also fine mimics. There is no evidence, however, that such birds understand what they are saying.

Grasshoppers and crickets use their legs to leap and make sounds.

1. Hold the backbone of the comb firmly in one hand. Try not to touch the teeth, or they will not vibrate freely.

2. Scrape an item along the teeth so that the teeth bend and spring back. Try moving the item fast, then slowly. Does the pitch of the sound change?

3. Try other combs. Do combs with long or short teeth give the highest note? Which type of items gives the loudest sounds?

MAKING SOUNDS

People have made sounds from the earliest times, from prehistoric grunts and yells to the millions of words in the two thousand or so languages of the modern world. Mammals and birds make sounds in a way similar to humans, using the voice box in their throats. Sound-producing devices have existed through the ages — from ancient, simple musical instruments, such as drums and pipes, to today's stereos and electronic instruments.

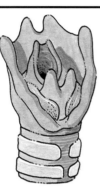

Vocal cords

Vocal cords pulled together and stretched to vibrate and make sounds.

Vocal cords apart for normal breathing.

*This cut-away view of the head and neck (far left) shows the voice box, or **larynx**, in position. The close-up views show the voice box making sounds and breathing normally.*

People with hearing problems may not hear their own voices, which can make it hard for them to learn to speak. It can help if they feel the voice box vibrations from another person, then feel their own voice box to copy the vibrations by making the same sounds.

A familiar sound is the human voice. It comes from the voice box or larynx in the neck. This hollow chamber, located at the base of the throat and top of the windpipe, has two pearl-white folds that stick out from its sides. They are the vocal folds, usually called the vocal cords. They vibrate along their free edge, rather than being string-like cords that are free to vibrate along their lengths.

In normal breathing, the vocal cords are held apart by muscles of the larynx. To speak, the muscles pull the cords near each other and stretch them slightly.

FAMOUS FIRSTS

THE ARMONICA
People have invented many musical instruments over the years, but not all have been successful. In the 1760s, American scientist and statesman Benjamin Franklin devised the armonica. Its different-sized glass bowls revolved on a central spindle. The rim of each bowl was touched to make a delicate humming note *(like the wine glasses on page 21)*. Beethoven and Mozart wrote music for the armonica, but the instrument was difficult to tune and transport. It gradually fell out of fashion.

Benjamin Franklin (1706-1790) is well known for his experiments with static electricity.

SPECIAL FX

FEEL YOUR VOICE
Your vocal cords vibrate to make sounds that emerge from your mouth and nose as sound waves. If these hit a flexible surface, they pass on their vibrations to it. This experiment uses a balloon as the flexible surface.

You need
A balloon, a friend.

1. Blow up the balloon quite large, but not too hard. Hold it lightly between your fingertips, 2 inches (5 cm) in front of your mouth. Have your friend lightly touch its other side.

2. Hum, talk, or make some other loud noise. Your sound waves hit the balloon and make it vibrate. The vibrations pass through the rubbery skin, and both you and your friend should feel them.

FUNNY CORDS, FUNNY VOICES
There are many methods of discovering how the human voice works. Here are a few of them. Can you think of others?

You need
Balloon, long blade of grass, whoopee cushion, plastic hair comb, and tracing or wax paper.

Stretch the neck wider or loosen it. The pitch of the squeal should change like your vocal cords.

1. Hold the long, flat blade of grass between your thumbs, as shown. Put your thumbs to your lips and blow through.

Small air gap along each side of blade.

2. The grass should vibrate with a buzz or hum. Try arching your thumbs slightly more or less, to change the air gap and stretch or loosen the blade for better results.

3. Fold a piece of tracing or wax paper in half. Place the teeth of the comb in the fold.

4. Press your lips gently onto the paper, and hum or blow. The paper vibrates between your lips and the comb teeth below. To play a tune, vary the pitch of your hum.

5. Blow up a balloon. Hold the neck firmly between your thumb and fingers of each hand.

6. Let air out slowly. You should hear a squealing sound as the two sides of the neck vibrate. This works like your vocal cords. The filled balloon is like your lungs, pushing air past the vocal cords.

7. Gently inflate a whoopee cushion. Then press or sit on it to expel the air.

8. Hear and see how the whoopee cushion neck vibrates to produce a sound. The vibrations are much slower than those of the balloon neck, so the pitch of the sound is far lower.

Can you play a tune by blowing over paper on a comb?

- The trademark symbol known as "His Master's Voice" for RCA Victor (Record Company of America) shows a dog listening to a record playing on an old-style gramophone. The original painting of "His Master's Voice" was done by Francis Barraud in 1900 from an actual scene. The dog's owner had made a recording of his voice. After the man died, the dog would sit and listen attentively to the voice coming from the horn of the gramophone.

- The loudest natural sounds ever made on Earth are probably gigantic volcanic eruptions, such as the explosion of the island of Krakatoa *(see page 24).*

- Some of the loudest sounds produced by human invention are the ones made by space rockets blasting from the launch pad. *Saturn V* rockets were a part of America's Apollo Moon missions of 1968-1972. They had their greatest success when *Apollo 11* landed silently on the Moon — an airless and therefore completely quiet place — on July 20, 1969. Once a rocket has taken off and enters the vacuum of space, it becomes totally silent.

Radios began to appear in many homes in the 1920s. The loudspeaker was large and heavy. It was often muffled and dull-sounding compared to today's versions.

Air flows up from the lungs, through the thin gap between the cords, and makes them vibrate rapidly back and forth. These vibrations shake the air around them, setting up sound waves that travel with the air, up and out through the mouth. The sounds from the vocal cords themselves are quiet and lack feature. They are given extra volume and character by the throat, the insides of the mouth and nose, and the air-filled chambers called sinuses inside the skull bones. This is what makes your own voice unique among thousands of others. The sounds are shaped into words and other recognizable utterances by the movements of the jaws, teeth, cheeks, tongue, and lips. To make higher notes, muscles in the larynx pull the cords longer and tighter, so they vibrate at higher frequencies.

Most musical instruments work in a similar way. The vibrating string of a piano or guitar, or the vibrating body and the air inside a trumpet or tuba, produce sound waves. These travel outward in all directions through the air until they are absorbed, reflected, or dampened (stopped).

Human voices and musical instruments are mechanical sound-makers. They produce sound waves from **kinetic energy**, the energy of motion. Sound is also

SPECIAL FX

THE SIMPLE LOUDSPEAKER
A loudspeaker works because of electricity *(see page 22)*. You can make a simple version that works mechanically.

You need
Plastic funnel, tracing paper, tape or rubber band, plastic hair comb.

1. Tape or rubber band the paper over the wide end of the funnel so that the paper is taut.

2. Scrape the teeth of the comb across the pointed end. Listen at the wide end. The vibrations of the comb's teeth scraping on the plastic travel to the paper. The paper vibrates, like the cone of a loudspeaker, sending sound waves into the air. Can you see the paper moving?

DIY SCIENCE

RINGING THE BELL
An electric bell uses the effects of magnetism and a "make-and-break" switch to make the clapper hit the tin-can bell very fast, producing a ringing sound.

1. Drill a hole in one wood block for a large bolt. Push the bolt through the hole, as shown. Glue and screw all blocks in position on the plank.

2. Wind some wire in a coil around the bolt, and leave two long ends. When electricity flows, it will turn the bolt into a magnet.

3. Bend, drill, and screw two metal strips to the middle block, as shown. The shorter strip is a contact. The longer strip is the bell clapper; position this close to the large bolt, but not touching it. Put a small bolt in the strip's free end. Screw down the battery holder, as shown.

You need
Small wood plank and wood blocks, insulated electrical wire, metal strips, bolts with nuts (small and large), tin can, battery (C, D, or 9-volt), battery holder, glue, wood screws, doorbell button.

This project requires an adult to do work and fill in additional instructions.

4. Glue a small nut to the block top, as shown. Screw a small bolt into it, so it just touches the short metal strip. Glue the can near the end of the clapper.

PLAY A DELICATE TUNE
Wineglasses are delicate. They may crack or break with the risk of cuts, so you need an adult's help.

You need
Eight wineglasses, water, flat tabletop, an adult.

1. Place the glasses in a row. Put a little water into one. Secure its base with one hand. Dip a fingertip of the other hand in the water, and stroke it gently around the rim.

2. Alter the speed and pressure of the rubbing. The glass should vibrate to produce an eerie, delicate humming sound.

3. Put increasing amounts of water in the glasses. Alter these so that the glasses play the notes of a musical scale *(see page 45).* Practice playing songs!

Hold the base, not the top, or this will reduce the vibrations.

- Thin-glass goblets vibrate when hit by sound waves. This is due to resonance *(see page 32).* Some singers listen to the note produced when a glass is tapped and then sing the same note back toward the glass. This may vibrate the glass enough to make it shatter.

- The same thing may happen to glass windows if they are vibrated by sound waves. In one church, the loud clang of a large bell shattered the stained-glass window above the altar.

5. Attach one end of the coil wire to a battery terminal. Attach the other end of the coil wire to the metal strips. Attach another wire to the smaller bolt; attach its other end to the doorbell button. Use another wire to attach the doorbell button to the other battery terminal.

6. Electricity flows in a circuit. When you press the doorbell button, the large bolt becomes a magnet and attracts the metal strips. They pull across, clang the bell, and break the circuit at the smaller bolt. The magnetism stops; the metal strips spring back and reconnect the circuit. The cycle repeats to give a ringing sound.

Bend the clapper so it hits the bell clearly.

Turn the small bolt to adjust the make-and-break switch for the best effect.

*In a stadium rock concert, the human voice would be too weak to hear by itself. It is made louder by electrical **amplification**.*

a form of energy, so the kinetic energy is transformed, or converted, into sound energy. However, sound is a fairly weak type of energy compared to heat, electricity, and other forms. If you could collect all the energy in the cheering and clapping sounds made by a huge crowd at a sports event, there would be hardly enough heat to boil a kettle of water.

Today, we have other ways of making sounds. The main one is the loudspeaker, used in tape players, television sets, stereos, and other kinds of audio equipment as the final link to turn electricity into sound. It uses the principle of **electromagnetism**. A varying pattern of electricity passes through a wire coil. This turns the coil into an electromagnet, whose magnetism interferes with a nearby magnet. The two magnets alternately attract and repel each other, making the coil move, or vibrate. It is attached to a cone shape of cardboard or plastic, and this vibrates

The loudspeaker's cone is attached to a coil of wire around or inside a strong magnet. Varying amounts of electricity flow through the wire, representing the patterns of sound. This turns the coil into a varying electromagnet, which vibrates as it is moved by the permanent magnet. The moving coil makes the cone vibrate and send out sound waves.

FAMOUS FIRSTS

THE ORCHESTRAL SOUNDMAKERS
Some of the musical instruments in an orchestra have changed over the years as newer types replaced older ones. The instruments have been modified over the years and even the centuries.

The basic trumpet shape was devised by ancient Egyptians over three thousand years ago. It was short and straight, with no valves (keys). The tube became longer and looped around in an oval during the fifteenth century. The valves were added in the 1820s.

The clarinet has a vibrating strip, called a reed, in the mouthpiece. It was first made about 1710 by Jacob Denner in Nuremberg, Germany, but did not become popular until about 1750.

In today's symphony orchestra, each group of instruments has a standard position. This provides the best overall combination of sound.

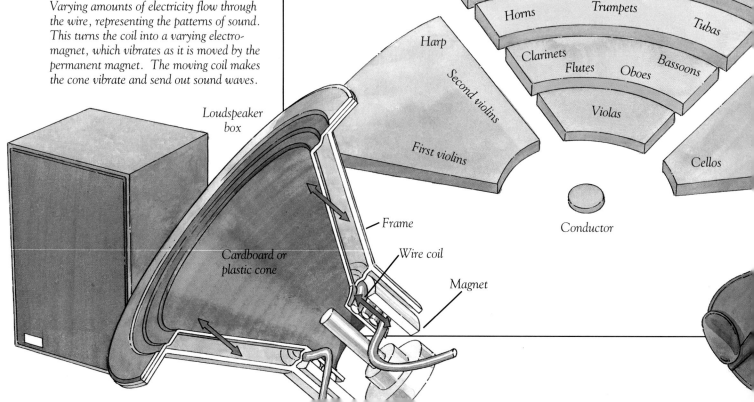

Loudspeaker box

Cardboard or plastic cone

Frame

Wire coil

Magnet

Percussion — Tympani — Trombo[ne]
Horns — Trumpets — Tubas
Harp — Clarinets — Flutes — Oboes — Bassoons
Second violins — Violas
First violins — Cellos
Conductor

The earliest harps were played in Sumeria over four thousand years ago. This stringed instrument has been made in many sizes and designs around the world. The modern harp was designed by Erard, the French company of piano- and harp-makers about 1810.

The piano's forerunner was the harpsichord, in which the strings were plucked. A piano's strings are struck by felt hammers. Its full name is pianoforte, and the first versions were made in 1698 by Bartolomeo Cristofori in Florence, Italy. The piano was improved over the years in Germany, Austria, England, and the United States.

The modern violin, with four strings, came into being about 1510. It was developed from two similar medieval instruments, the fiddle and the rebec. The strings are vibrated by a bow.

DIY SCIENCE

THE TWANGING GUITAR
A vibrating string changes pitch with changing length.

You need
Ruler, pencils, rubber bands of various thicknesses.

1. Stretch a rubber band over a ruler. Slide a pencil under the band at each end of the ruler, so the band's middle part can vibrate freely. Pluck the band. Listen to its note. Slide the pencils closer together, so the vibrating part of the band is shorter. Pluck again. Has the note changed?

2. Using the scale on the ruler, contrast the notes from a certain length of band — 10 inches (26 cm) — with the note from half this length — 5 inches (13 cm). Does one note sound twice as high as the other? *(See page 33.)*

3. Try other thicknesses of rubber bands and vary their tension. When bands of the same length are twanged, does a thicker band make a note different from a thinner one?

FASCINATING FACTS

- Three original pianos built by the inventor Bartolomeo Cristofori still survive. The oldest, dated 1720, is in New York City. The others are in Rome, Italy (1722) and Leipzig, Germany (1726).

- A few musical instruments are named after their inventors. From the 1840s came the saxophone, named after Belgian instrument-maker Adolphe Sax. Another is the sousaphone of 1898, named after the American marching-band music composer John Philip Sousa. The modern moog electronic synthesizer was first made in 1964 by American electronics expert Robert Moog.

- Some musical instruments have developed from devices used originally to send sound signals to communicate over lengthy distances. Some of the best examples are drums and horns.

- Some composers have written musical works for very unusual instruments. There have been several "junkyard" concertos featuring sounds such as banging car doors, blaring car horns, the thumping of empty oil drums, clanking chains, the crunch of a car-crusher, and the deep throb of a bulldozer's diesel engine.

- One musical piece has no sounds at all. It is called *4 minutes 33 seconds*. It was written by the American composer John Cage in 1954. A pianist sits at the piano and plays nothing for exactly 4 minutes and 33 seconds.

- In the Alps of Europe, the long wooden trumpet called the alphorn was used by herdsmen to call each other. Also called the alphenhorn and alpine horn, its loud, deep trumpeting sound echoed across the valleys and summoned people to church — or to war. Similar instruments were used in upland regions of Germany, Scandinavia, and Eastern Europe.

In 1883, a volcano erupted on the small island of Krakatoa near Sumatra in southeast Asia. The island blew apart and disappeared. The immense roar of the eruption was heard 1,865 miles (3,000 km) away. It was the loudest sound ever recorded.

too, sending out sound waves into the air. Earphones use a similar, but much smaller, device or one based on crystals that vibrate as the varying electricity goes through them.

Loudspeakers did not become available until the 1910s. They required the right piece of electrical equipment — the **triode**, or amplifying valve — invented by American Lee Forest in 1906. This boosted the electricity. Today, sound can be produced first in electrical form. Examples are the electrical guitar and the synthesizer. In addition, sound waves can be changed into electricity by the microphone (*see page 28*). Most manipulation of sound, such as the manipulation done in a recording studio, is now accomplished while it is in patterns of electric currents. The loudspeaker then turns it back into sound waves.

FAMOUS FIRSTS

THROUGH THE SOUND BARRIER
The speed of sound in air varies with temperature and height, slowing to about 660 miles (1,062 km) per hour at high altitudes. The first person to go faster than sound was Charles Yeager. On October 14, 1947, he flew the rocket-engined Bell X-1 to 670 miles (1,078 km) per hour at an altitude of 41,997 feet (12,800 m). People feared the plane would shake and fall to bits as it tried to break the sound barrier. But all went smoothly, and the sound barrier was no barrier at all.

The orange Bell X-1, nicknamed Glamorous Glennis *after Yeager's wife, was launched from under a B-29 Superfortress bomber at a height of 11,812 feet (3,600 m).*

FAMOUS FIRSTS

ELECTRIC INSTRUMENTS
Musicians use microphones, amplifiers, and loudspeakers to pick up the sounds of instruments and make them louder. The first popular instrument to be based on electricity was the electric guitar. The metal strings vibrate near what is known as a pick-up, a magnet with a coil of wire around it. The shaking string disturbs the magnetism, and this alters the electric current. The earliest electric guitars were made in the 1930s.

Fender Broadcaster was an early mass-produced electric guitar with a solid body (1950).

The keyboard of an electric organ produces electrical signals, not sounds. Loudspeakers turn the electricity into sound.

Magnetic pick-ups

DIY SCIENCE

SOUND MACHINE
You need
Cardboard tube, sheets of thin cardboard, plastic wrap, pencil, tape, rubber band, scissors.

1. Draw around the end of the tube onto the cardboard.

2. Cut out the resulting cardboard disk.

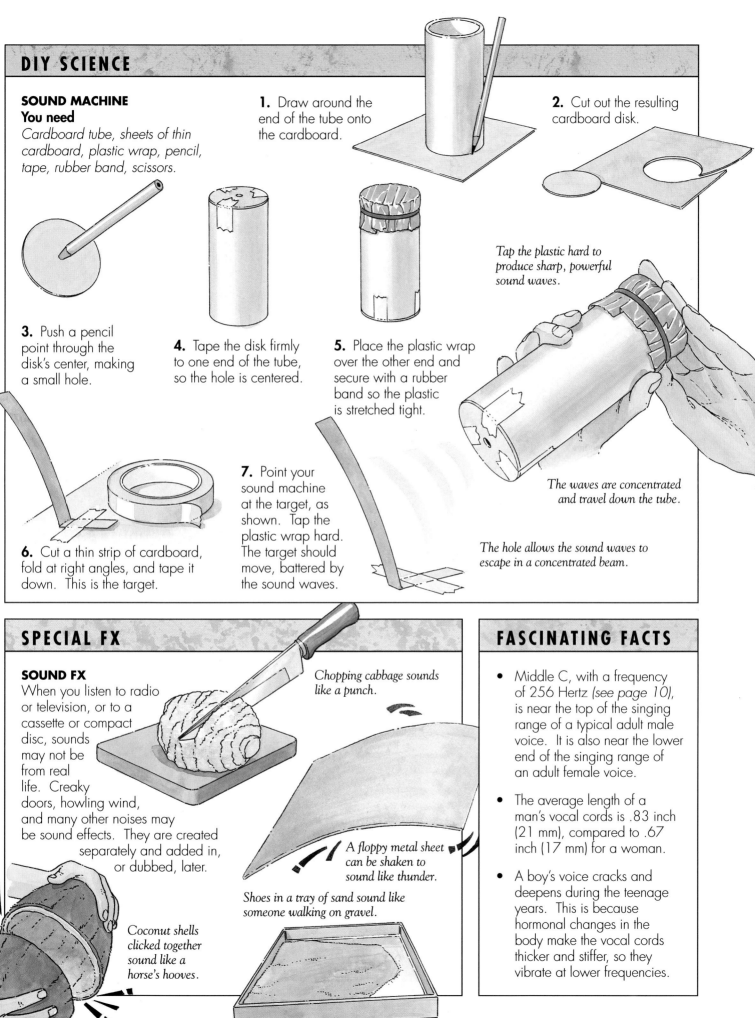

3. Push a pencil point through the disk's center, making a small hole.

4. Tape the disk firmly to one end of the tube, so the hole is centered.

5. Place the plastic wrap over the other end and secure with a rubber band so the plastic is stretched tight.

Tap the plastic hard to produce sharp, powerful sound waves.

6. Cut a thin strip of cardboard, fold at right angles, and tape it down. This is the target.

7. Point your sound machine at the target, as shown. Tap the plastic wrap hard. The target should move, battered by the sound waves.

The waves are concentrated and travel down the tube.

The hole allows the sound waves to escape in a concentrated beam.

SPECIAL FX

SOUND FX
When you listen to radio or television, or to a cassette or compact disc, sounds may not be from real life. Creaky doors, howling wind, and many other noises may be sound effects. They are created separately and added in, or dubbed, later.

Chopping cabbage sounds like a punch.

A floppy metal sheet can be shaken to sound like thunder.

Shoes in a tray of sand sound like someone walking on gravel.

Coconut shells clicked together sound like a horse's hooves.

FASCINATING FACTS

- Middle C, with a frequency of 256 Hertz *(see page 10)*, is near the top of the singing range of a typical adult male voice. It is also near the lower end of the singing range of an adult female voice.

- The average length of a man's vocal cords is .83 inch (21 mm), compared to .67 inch (17 mm) for a woman.

- A boy's voice cracks and deepens during the teenage years. This is because hormonal changes in the body make the vocal cords thicker and stiffer, so they vibrate at lower frequencies.

The outer ear flap collects sound waves and funnels them toward the eardrum. This thin, flexible membrane vibrates as sound waves hit it. The vibrations pass along a chain of three tiny bones, called the ossicles, to the snail-shaped cochlea. Inside the cochlea, the vibrations produce ripples in a fluid, which are turned into electrical nerve signals.

DETECTING SOUNDS

The two sound receivers on either side of the human head are incredibly sensitive at detecting sound waves. They can adapt instantly from straining to hear a whisper to coping with a jet plane roaring overhead. But our ears have their limits. All around us is an ocean of invisible sound — we only hear some of it.

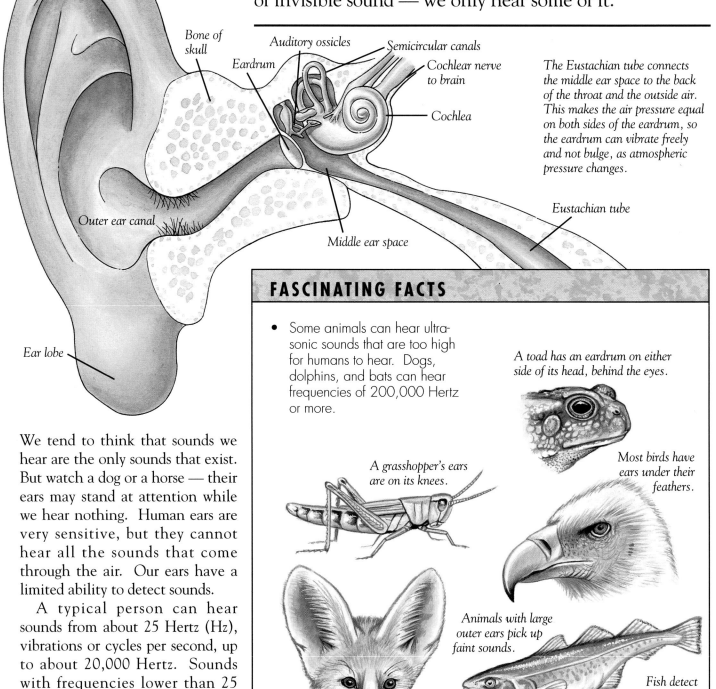

Outer ear flap

Bone of skull

Auditory ossicles

Eardrum

Semicircular canals

Cochlear nerve to brain

Cochlea

Outer ear canal

Middle ear space

Ear lobe

The Eustachian tube connects the middle ear space to the back of the throat and the outside air. This makes the air pressure equal on both sides of the eardrum, so the eardrum can vibrate freely and not bulge, as atmospheric pressure changes.

Eustachian tube

We tend to think that sounds we hear are the only sounds that exist. But watch a dog or a horse — their ears may stand at attention while we hear nothing. Human ears are very sensitive, but they cannot hear all the sounds that come through the air. Our ears have a limited ability to detect sounds.

A typical person can hear sounds from about 25 Hertz (Hz), vibrations or cycles per second, up to about 20,000 Hertz. Sounds with frequencies lower than 25 Hertz do not stimulate the ear, so we are unaware of them. Yet they do exist, and some animals can

FASCINATING FACTS

- Some animals can hear ultrasonic sounds that are too high for humans to hear. Dogs, dolphins, and bats can hear frequencies of 200,000 Hertz or more.

A toad has an eardrum on either side of its head, behind the eyes.

A grasshopper's ears are on its knees.

Most birds have ears under their feathers.

Animals with large outer ears pick up faint sounds.

Fish detect vibrations with the silvery lateral line along the middle of the body.

HOW THE EAR HEARS
This model ear works in a similar way to the real human ear.

You need
Thick and thin cardboard, bendable drinking straw, Ping-Pong ball, side part only of a cake pan, plastic wrap, glue, tape, bowl of water, pencil, scissors, adult supervision.

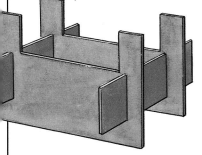

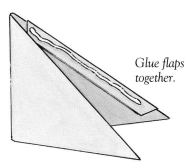

1. Draw around one-quarter of the pan onto a rectangle of thick cardboard, and cut the piece out. Do the same for a second piece. Carefully cut slots in the cut-out rectangles for two cross-pieces, as shown.

Glue flaps together.

2. Tape or glue the cross-pieces in place, as shown. This will be a stand for the cake pan.

3. Stretch the plastic wrap over the pan so that it is taut with no creases or tears. Tape the film in place, taking care not to poke or stretch it. This is the eardrum.

4. Carefully cut and bend a sheet of thin cardboard to make a double-folded triangle, as shown. Fold back the two long edges and glue them so that the cardboard triangle is open on one side only.

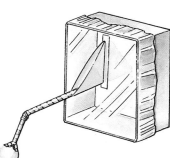

5. Carefully cut open one end of the straw nearest the bendable part. Push it onto the Ping-Pong ball and tape it in place. Glue or tape the other end into the folded triangle, as shown.

6. Tape the triangle on to the plastic wrap with cardboard strips, with the straw at the center. The straw acts like a lever to enlarge vibrations in the same way as the ossicle bones do in the ear.

7. Place the pan on the stand near the bowl of water. Adjust the straw so the ball just dips in the water. Shout at the model eardrum. Sound waves hit it and make it vibrate, which causes the ball to vibrate, too. This produces ripples in the water, like the ripples in the fluid of the ear's cochlea.

Try sounds of different volume and pitch. Do they produce different types of ripples?

SPECIAL FX

DIRECTION OF SOUND
Sounds reaching you from the side are louder in one ear than in the other. Because sound waves travel slowly, they reach the closest ear before the farther one. The brain adjusts for volume and time differences to locate a sound's source. Blindfold a friend, and make sounds from various positions. Have the friend guess the direction the sound is coming from.

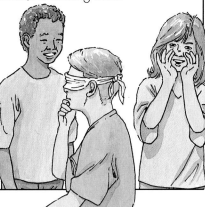

27

detect them. .Sounds above 20,000 Hertz do not affect our ears, although they may be heard by animals. Sounds too low for our hearing range are known as **infrasound**, while those that are too high are called **ultrasound**.

Ears detect sounds but do not process them. The ear converts the energy of sound waves into the energy of patterns of tiny electrical signals called nerve impulses. These go along nerves to the brain and reach the parts of the brain called auditory centers. There, the patterns of nerve impulses are sorted and processed, compared with information in the brain's memory, and passed to the conscious, thinking centers of the brain. The result is you become aware of the sounds and are able to identify them — or not!

A microphone works in a similar way to the ear. It also converts patterns of sound waves into corresponding patterns of

The moving-coil microphone has a diaphragm membrane, like an eardrum, that vibrates from sound waves. This makes a coil of wire move in a magnetic field, which alters the pattern of electricity flowing through the wire.

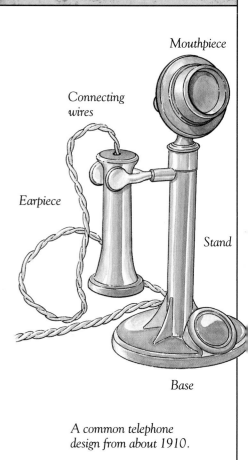

FAMOUS FIRSTS

TALKING BY TELEPHONE

From the 1840s, people could communicate across long distances by sending electrical signals along wires by telegraph. Scottish-born American scientist Alexander Graham Bell (1847-1922) wanted to find a way to send the sounds of speech, rather than the dot-dash system of Morse code, across distances. He finally succeeded in 1876 with his "speaking telegraph." It used the electromagnetic effect, similar to that of the modern microphone. A diaphragm attached to a coil of wire vibrated the wire in a magnetic field, creating a pattern of electric current that copied the pattern of sound waves. The transmitter (mouthpiece) and receiver (earpiece) of Bell's first telephone were almost the same device, but they worked in opposite ways.

Mouthpiece

Connecting wires

Earpiece

Stand

Base

A common telephone design from about 1910.

FAMOUS FIRSTS

THE EAR OF THE TELEPHONE

Once Bell had produced his early telephones, the American inventor Thomas Edison (1847-1931) devised his own version. Edison's differed in the mouthpiece, which is the microphone of the telephone. His version had a small container or capsule of tiny grains of carbon. Electricity passed through it. Sound waves hit a diaphragm attached to the capsule, and squashed or stretched the grains. This altered the amount of electricity passing through in a pattern that represented the sound waves. Edison's carbon-button basic design is still used in many telephones today.

Diaphragm

Carbon granules

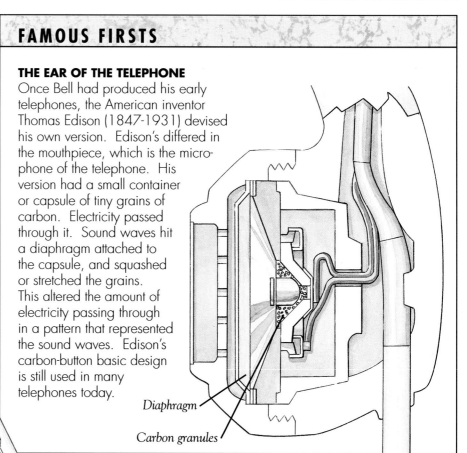

Protective cover

Microphone mechanism

DIY SCIENCE

STRINGING WORDS TOGETHER

The vibrations of sound pass through liquids and solids, as well as the gases in air. Make a telephone to find out for yourself.

You need

Selection of cup-shaped items, such as a thin plastic cup, thick plastic cup, Styrofoam cup, and cardboard toilet tissue tube; selection of strings and threads, such as cotton thread, woolen yarn, natural string, plastic twine, and fishing line; scissors, friend, adult supervision.

1. You can also make your own cups by stretching plastic wrap over a cardboard tube and taping it in place. Try the same with a plastic or wooden tube, too.

Make a cup out of a cardboard tube.

2. With the scissors point, make a tiny hole in the base of each cup. Pull the string through this, and tie a large knot. Or tie the string around a paper clip, and pull this flat onto the cup's base.

3. Do the same with a second cup, leaving about 10 feet (3 m) of string between the cups.

Sound waves from voice make cup vibrate.

4. You and a friend should each hold a cup, as shown. Stand together, and let the string flop onto the ground. Speak into your cup while your friend listens into the other cup.

5. Now step farther apart, and pull the string taut. Speak and listen as in step 4.

Make a hole in base of cup.

Does the telephone work best with the string loose or taut?

6. Have your friend speak into the cup, while you listen to yours. It helps if you say "over" each time you finish and expect a reply. Otherwise, what happens if you both speak at once?

7. Make different versions of the telephone using different cups and strings. Which work best? Are the results improved when you pull the string as taut as possible?

FASCINATING FACTS

- Stage performers sometimes use a microphone on a stand. The microphone "hears" their voices and instruments and feeds the electrical signals into the main amplification or PA (public address) system. The sounds can also be picked up by microphones along the front of the stage.

- At some performances, there may be over a hundred microphones for singers, instruments, sound effects, and even audience noise. The signals from them are combined at a large mixing board operated by sound engineers.

At important press events of the past, each radio and television station and newspaper team had a large microphone to detect the speaker's voice. Today, they usually agree to share a few small microphones.

electrical signals. These travel along a wire to an amplifier that makes the signals stronger. The electrical signals can be altered by various means, such as boosting low frequencies and then feeding them into a loudspeaker or earphones so that they are turned back into sound waves.

Electrical amplification of sounds is common today — from battery-operated police bullhorns to the giant amplifiers and loudspeakers at a dance club or concert. The development of such amplification depended on the availability of suitable electrical equipment, including triode valves (*see page 24*) invented in the 1900s. Before this time, people had to rely on the natural loudness of their voices, musical instruments, bells, and other items that produce sound.

A vital feature of acoustics is resonance. Each object in the world has a natural frequency of vibration, from the human voice box to a wooden board and from a guitar body to a bell. The frequency of vibration depends on the object's size and shape, the thickness and flexibility of its material, how much air it encloses, and many other factors. When struck or shaken, the object vibrates at its natural resonant frequency and so produces sounds of a certain pitch.

A sound's intensity, similar to loudness or volume, is measured in "bels," named after Alexander Graham Bell (see page 28). The bel is a very large unit, so the loudness scale is shown in decibels (dB equals one-tenth of a bel). Noises greater than 85 decibels can harm the ears.

DIY SCIENCE

HEAR AND BE HEARD!

The megaphone and the ear trumpet both work in the same way. They are not electrical, so they cannot increase the total volume of a sound. But they can collect and funnel sound waves, concentrating them like a lens focuses a light beam. The sounds become louder where you want them, and quieter elsewhere.

You need
Two large sheets of strong cardboard, tape, tape measure, quiet place, friend.

1. Roll the cardboard into a funnel shape, with a 2-inch (5-cm) hole at the small end. Tape firmly. Repeat with the other cardboard.

2. Stand 6 feet (2 m) from your friend. Speak in your normal voice, reciting a phrase or a saying. Have the friend walk away slowly and signal when he or she can no longer hear you. Measure the distance between the two of you.

3. Repeat step 2 with your voice at the same volume and tone. But use the cardboard funnel as if it were a megaphone. When you speak through it, the sound waves are beamed directly toward your friend. Can the friend hear you at a greater distance?

4. Repeat step 2 without your megaphone. Have your friend use the cardboard funnel as an ear trumpet.

5. Repeat a final time, you with the megaphone and your friend with the ear trumpet. Does this give the maximum distance?

0 dB Silence   *10 dB Distant leaves rustling*   *20 dB Watch ticking*   *30 dB Your bedroom at night*   *40 dB Quiet classroom at exam time*   *50 dB On the bank of a brook or stream*

SPECIAL FX

CHLADNI FIGURES
German scientist Ernst Chladni (1756-1827) experimented with the vibrations produced by sound waves. He scattered sand or sugar grains on very thin metal plates and vibrated the plates with sound waves. The grains made intricate patterns on the plates, depending on which parts vibrated (according to the pitch and volume of the sound). The patterns are called Chladni figures. Modern versions of them are used to study the acoustic properties of musical instruments, loudspeakers, wall panels, windows, and many other objects.

The sound waves of a human voice saying "aah" made this thin, circular plate vibrate. The tiny, light grains on it took on a petal-like shape — one of many Chladni patterns.

FAMOUS FIRSTS

THE MYSTERY OF THE CRYSTAL
Crystals have many unusual properties. For example, they allow electricity to pass through them but, if they are squeezed or stretched, they alter the amount of electricity. A crystal, such as quartz, that is squeezed hard can generate electricity. The opposite also happens. By passing varying amounts of electricity through a crystal, the crystal changes its shape accordingly. This is the piezoelectric effect, discovered in 1880 by Pierre Curie (1859-1906) and his brother Jacques. It is used in various sound devices. For example, a fast-changing electric current passed through a crystal makes the crystal vibrate. If it is attached to a diaphragm membrane, the vibrations produce sounds, especially ultrasound. The piezoelectric effect is also used in some microphones and headphones.

Most high-quality microphones are moving coil, not crystal.

FASCINATING FACTS

- The first electrical hearing aid was invented in the United States by Millar Hutchinson in 1902.

- Ear trumpets used in ancient Greece and Rome were crafted from metals and decorated with jewels.

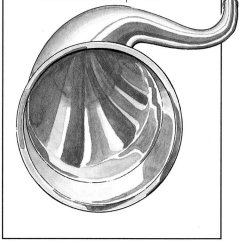

| ...dB People ...ing, about ...et (1 m) ...rt | 70 dB Hum of conversation before class | 80 dB Cars on a paved, main road | 90 dB Underground train at full speed | 100 dB Very loud dance club, exceeding legal noise limit | 110 dB Pneumatic hammer, if you were using it! | 120 dB Jet engine 30 feet (10 m) away |

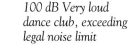

Musical instruments are designed and built to resonate well at certain frequencies. In effect, this makes them sound louder and produce purer tones at particular pitches.

Resonance can pass from one object to another. This is **sympathetic resonance**. It can be used to advantage in designing concert halls and studios. But it creates problems, too. In an orchestra when a solo is played, the sound waves emitted can set up sympathetic resonance in other instruments, such as cellos and drums, causing unwanted sound.

Many towns and cities are full of invisible pollution — noise. Continuous loud sounds of road vehicles, airplanes, trains, people, and machinery cause stress and various symptoms of illness, such as headaches. Some workers wear earplugs to protect their hearing. Noise meters measure the loudness in decibels.

DIY SCIENCE

THE GHOST GUITARIST
Resonance can be shown with two stringed instruments, such as a piano and guitar. Lean the guitar on a wall near the piano (not against it). Strike a piano key hard, let it sound for two seconds, then dampen it. Listen carefully to the guitar. Strike various piano keys. With certain notes, you hear the guitar strings vibrate, too. This is due to sympathetic resonance. Sound waves from the piano pass through the air, hit the guitar strings, and make the string of the same note vibrate. Does the distance between piano and guitar alter the effect?

FAMOUS FIRSTS

THE GREAT ORGANS
Traditional pipe organs are found in many churches, concert halls, and similar places. With this instrument, sound is made by air blowing through hollow pipes. The air and pipes vibrate. The pipes are resonators that enhance the notes. The bigger and longer the pipe, the deeper the note. The first pipe organs were mechanical versions of ancient pan pipes *(see page 44)*.

DIY SCIENCE

PROOF OF SOUNDPROOFING
Specially designed materials absorb sound and keep it away from where it is not wanted. This is called soundproofing. Check various materials for soundproofing qualities.

You need
Several identical cardboard boxes, loudspeaker, glue, tape, scissors, test materials (egg-boxes, cardboard, plastic foam, newspaper, cotton, an old rug or carpet, etc.).

DIY SCIENCE

ANALOG AND DIGITAL

An unfretted instrument, like a cello, represents an analog system. The quantities — in this case, string lengths — can be anything from 0 upward in very tiny steps. In theory, there is endless variation. A fretted instrument, like the guitar, illustrates the principle of a digital system. Different quantities — in this case, string lengths again — fit into a set and prearranged scale, for example 1, 2, 3 inches (cm) and so on. If a cellist were to copy a tune played by another cellist, small differences could creep in. However, the same process with a guitar, which has pre-made notes, is more likely to result in an exact copy.

Analog type — with no pre-set divisions. You can press anywhere.

Digital type — divisions of scale work like frets, showing where to press the band.

Make a digital guitar (like on page 23) with a scale (frets) showing where you press the rubber band, and an analog one without frets. Which is easier to play?

FASCINATING FACTS

- The noise from trucks can shake and damage nearby structures, such as buildings and bridges. The damage may come from sound waves through the air or from very low-frequency vibrations passing through the ground.

- The Concorde is the only passenger plane to fly faster than sound at 1,305 miles (2,100 km) per hour.

1. Line each box with the same thickness of a certain material, about 1 inch (3 cm) carefully cut to size, then glued or taped.

2. Place the loudspeaker on a flat, carpeted surface. Play a song in which the sounds are fairly constant in volume.

3. Put your various boxes one by one over the loudspeaker. Which quiets the sound the most? That material is best at absorbing sound waves.

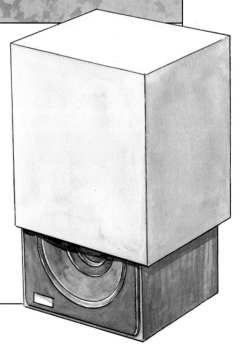

RECORDING SOUNDS

Recorded sound is part of life. We hear voices, music, and other sounds that have been stored on discs, tapes, and other equipment. We hear recorded sounds played on music systems, computers, televisions, and radios. Yet, about a hundred years ago, all sound was "live." It was produced by people talking, musicians, instruments, and machines.

In the 1850s, Alexander Bell, Sr., (Alexander Graham Bell's father) devised a system of symbols, called Visible Speech, for sounds. It helped people with speech and hearing problem

In 1877, British scientist John Strutt (Lord Rayleigh) published a book called *The Theory of Sound*, which he wrote partly while staying on a houseboat on the Nile River in Egypt. The book was a collection and summary of the current knowledge about sound. It described the nature of sound waves — how they are made and how they travel through various substances from gases to metals. It predicted future research, laying the foundations for the science of acoustics.

The same year saw the start of recorded and played-back sound. This era began with the words, "Mary had a little lamb." American inventor Thomas Edison and a machine-maker John Kreusi designed and made a machine called the phonograph. The inventors had the idea while working on another device, a "repeater" to repeat electrical telegraph messages. The phonograph was the first working device to record sounds in a physical form and play them back again. People were amazed by the invention. Until they experienced the phonograph for themselves, they could not believe that a machine could "hear" what they said and then "speak" it back to them.

DIY SCIENCE

SOUNDS IN THE BRAIN

Close your eyes and imagine your favorite piece of music. It might be an orchestral piece or a rap song. Try to remember all the details. Does it seem real? Now think of a close relative or friend. Imagine that they are speaking. Try to recall all the features of their pronunciation of words, which makes each voice seem unique. How do you imagine this? It does not happen in your ears, but in your brain — your "mind's ear." The human brain has an amazing ability to record many thousands of sounds as memories. It records not only the main features but also the tiny details. This is how you know when someone is impersonating another person's voice. Even the best impressionists cannot copy voices exactly. When you hear a sound with your ears and register it in your brain, you compare it at once with all the sounds stored in your memory banks. This is how you identify it. Like other memories of sights, birthdates, and word meanings, sound memories are probably stored as pathways through the billions of interlinked nerve cells in the brain. When a tiny electrical nerve signal flows around the pathway, it activates the memory and you hear the sound in your mind.

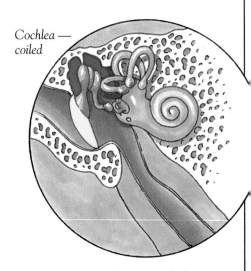

Cochlea — coiled

The tiny electrical nerve signals that represent sounds in the brain begin in the cochlea (see page 26). In reality, it is snail-shaped (above). Drawn in a straightened form (below), a long, flexible membrane can be seen. The membrane vibrates in response to sounds and generates nerve signals that travel along the auditory nerve to the brain.

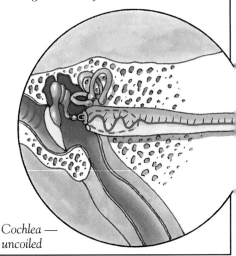

Cochlea — uncoiled

SPECIAL FX

WORDS FOR SOUNDS

Hiss! Boo! Ugh! Words like these are written versions of sounds and noises. The process of inventing words that sound like sounds and using them in speech and writing is called **onomatopoeia**. We have many onomatopoeic words, especially for animal sounds such as *woof, meow, baa,* and *moo.* Write a story containing as many of these words as possible.

SPECIAL FX

SOUNDS AND LETTER SHAPES

Look in a magazine or comic book at the photos, drawings, and advertisements. You will sometimes see words with specially designed shapes to make them look the way they sound. They are onomatopoeic words. Make up your own letter designs and word shapes using extra lines, shading, stars, and shapes to emphasize the way a word is pronounced.

FASCINATING FACTS

SIGNS FOR SPEECH

No animals can copy the sounds of human speech and understand their meaning — not even the highly intelligent chimpanzees. Although their voice box and brain are not adapted to do this, chimps can learn to understand messages and "speak" in a silent way with sign language. They make signs with their hands and put together simple sentences such as "Food, me, give!"

Some people communicate by sight, not sound, using sign language for letters, words, and phrases. This is useful for people who cannot hear or speak clearly.

The original phonograph stored or recorded sound in the form of a groove. A metal point called the stylus pressed a groove in a layer of tinfoil that covered a brass cylinder. This was a mechanical system of moving parts and so did not use electricity.

Other inventors soon improved the quality of the recordings by replacing the foil with hard wax, in which the metal stylus cut a groove. In 1888, Emile Berliner introduced a flat disk instead of a cylinder. He also devised a method whereby the stylus moved from side to side, rather than up and down like Edison's original system. By 1904, Berliner had made an improved version that could be mass produced to a high-quality standard. The concept of the "record" was born. During the

The first tape recorders of the 1930s had two separate large reels of wide tape and were very bulky. In 1980, the Sony Corporation introduced the first Walkman, which played cassettes. People could then listen to recorded sound virtually anywhere.

FAMOUS FIRSTS

EDISON'S PHONOGRAPH
The original phonograph both recorded sounds and played them back. Sound waves funneled into the mouthpiece and bounced off a flexible, thin, metal sheet (the diaphragm) and made it vibrate. The diaphragm passed its vibrations to a steel needle, the stylus. The stylus pressed a groove of varying depth in tinfoil that covered a brass cylinder, which was being turned by hand. After a recording was made, the stylus was moved back to the beginning and the cylinder was turned again. The process reversed and sent out sound waves from the funnel. One of the very first recordings was Edison reciting "Mary had a little lamb."

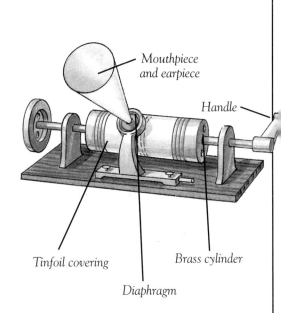

Mouthpiece and earpiece

Handle

Tinfoil covering

Brass cylinder

Diaphragm

Thomas Alva Edison (1847-1931) invented many things that changed daily life, including improved versions of the telephone, early motion picture equipment, and the electric light bulb.

FAMOUS FIRSTS

TAPE RECORDERS
The first system to store sound through the use of magnetism was invented by Vlademar Poulsen in about 1898 in Denmark. It used long, thin steel wire. The first tape machine was the German Magnetophon of 1936. It used a flexible cellulose tape with a thin coat of magnetic powder. The Philips company sold the first cassettes in 1963. They were small and convenient, but not high-fidelity. Cassettes with chrome coatings, and then other metal combinations, plus the Dolby noise-reduction system greatly improved their quality.

OLD-TIME MUSIC

Find an old "78" record that is no longer wanted, and rotate it on a turntable. Carefully push a long pin through the middle of the base of a thin plastic cup so the point sticks out below. Tape the pin to the cup base. Hold the cup rim by your fingertips, and press the pinpoint at an angle in a groove of the record. The vibrations pass up the length of the pin to the cup, which sends out sound waves.

Pin in groove

HEARING YOUR OWN VOICE

Sound waves from your voice box are picked up by your ears. Voice box vibrations also pass through the bones and flesh of your neck and head to your inner ears. So your ears receive two sets of vibrations from your voice compared to the single set of sound waves heard by others. This is why your recorded voice sounds different to you because just one set of vibrations is recorded and played back on the tape.

Place a microphone in different positions — against your neck and skull — to record the different sounds of your voice.

FASCINATING FACTS

• Emile Berliner's first flat-disk records were made of hard rubber. This was followed by shellac, a resin-type substance originally obtained from certain insects. Eventually plastics were tried, including vinyl.

• Various improvements to the flat disk led to 10-inch and 12-inch diameter versions, rotating at 78 rpm (revolutions per minute).

• Longer periods of music and other sounds (over thirty minutes on each side) came about in 1948 with the arrival of the vinyl LP, or long-playing record. Its microgrooves were much thinner, and the disk rotated slower at 33 rpm.

• The single, or 45, rotated at 45 rpm. It had only a few minutes of sound on each side. But single records were inexpensive to make, and many people could afford to buy them. This led to jukebox records starting in the 1940s and "Top Ten" charts starting in the 1950s.

12-inch LP (33 rpm)

10-inch record (78 rpm)

7-inch single (45 rpm)

early 1900s, the first commercial recordings were made of singers, musicians, and speakers.

The invention of the triode valve (*see page 24*) to enlarge, or amplify, electrical signals meant that sounds could be made louder electrically. Microphones and loudspeakers were developed and, in the 1920s, sound-recording systems changed from purely mechanical to electrical. Gramophones, or record players, found their way into many homes. Recorded sound became part of everyday life.

Beginning in the 1930s, sound was also recorded as tiny patches of magnetism on flexible tape. The 1980s saw another form of recording arise — the compact disc. A CD's microscopic pits are read by a laser beam. Sounds are also stored in the form of magnetic patches on computer disks and in the solid-state chips of computer memory circuits.

(see page 24)
(see page 22)

FAMOUS FIRSTS

The first movies were "silent." There were no sounds recorded with the pictures. However, musicians in the movie theater sometimes played an accompaniment as the film was shown. The first "talkie" was *The Jazz Singer* starring Al Jolson in 1927. Sounds were recorded at the same time as the pictures, and both were played back together. Jolson spoke and sang for part of the movie. The first film with complete accompanying sound, or a soundtrack, was *Lights of New York* the following year.

A scene from the first talkie, The Jazz Singer. *Audiences were stunned to hear Jolson's voice, as though he were speaking directly to them. The silent film era was history within two years as the era of talkies began.*

Sounds are recorded on a CD as microscopic pits in a layer of shiny metal. When a compact disc is spun in a CD player, the pits either reflect or scatter light from a laser. The reflected light changes into sound.

Sounds are recorded on tape as microscopic patches of magnetism on flexible tape coated with iron oxide. The patches are detected by electromagnetism (see page 22) as the tape slides past a coil of wire in the recording head, and turned into electrical signals.

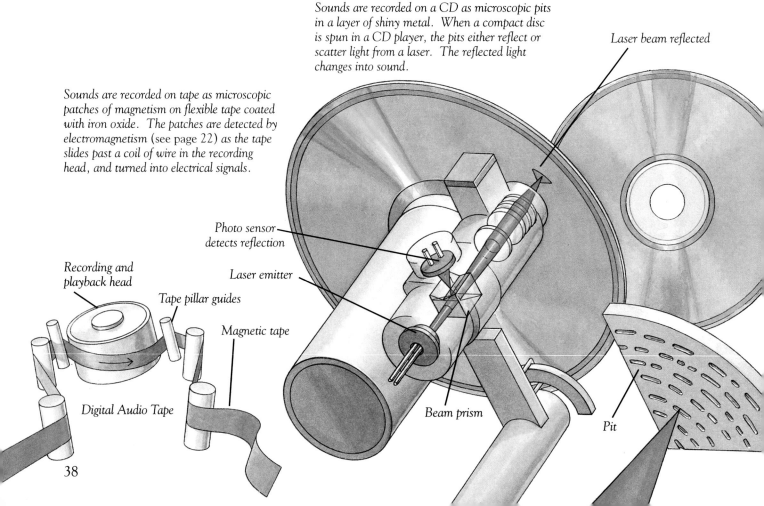

Laser beam reflected

Recording and playback head

Tape pillar guides

Photo sensor detects reflection

Laser emitter

Magnetic tape

Digital Audio Tape

Beam prism

Pit

SIGHT AND SOUND

The sounds that accompany motion pictures have been recorded in various ways. In 1894, Thomas Edison produced a simple system for playing back sounds from a phonograph to accompany the pictures from his kinetoscope. In the 1920s, the Vitaphone worked in a similar way with electrical signals linking or synchronizing the movie film and the phonograph disk. Next, the sounds were converted into electrical signals, which were then turned into a pattern of light and dark pulses. These were recorded on the film itself next to the pictures, as a wavy stripe called an optical soundtrack.

Videotape records the sound in the same form as it records pictures, as micro-patches of magnetism. Modern film also has a magnetic stripe along the side, to record the sound magnetically.

When movie frames are shown in a fast sequence, about twenty-five per second, the eyes blur them into one continuous scene of movement.

Recording slit
Recording lens
Light beam exposes film
Light valve
Lenses
Lamp

Optical soundtrack recorder

Feed spool
Lens
Take-up spool
Viewfinder
Capstan
Pressure roller
Sound head
Film gate

Super 8 home movie camera

Magnetic movie soundtrack player

Sound drum
Film from image-projector
Magnetic playback head
Film drive sprocket
Amplifier
Loudspeaker

DOLBY® NOISE REDUCTION

The Dolby noise reduction system uses electronic circuits to improve sound quality, especially for cassette tapes. The system selects and boosts certain high frequencies, which often include background "hiss." It then filters and reduces these and combines them with the rest of the sound. Dolby was devised in 1967 by American electrical engineer Ray Dolby. There are now several systems, including Dolby A, B, C and DBX, and Dolby Stereo for movie soundtracks.

- In fiber-optic cables, a voice on the telephone is coded as flashes of laser light. These pulse millions of times per second. In this way, light travels more efficiently than electricity in long cables.

- In the 1880s, Alexander Graham Bell worked on a fiber-optic device called the photophone, but it never became practical.

The photophone converted sounds to flashes of light.

39

USES FOR SOUND

Our lives are filled with sound. During a typical day, we may hear people talking, radios and televisions blaring, vehicles and machines running, thunder, wind, and rain. Now and again, we hear sounds that are out of the ordinary. They can startle, worry, or even frighten us. Other sounds, such as music, give us pleasure.

A baby's scream can be piercing. Nature has designed the baby's cry to be that way. Adult ears are very sensitive to the cries so that we respond and care for the baby.

It is a quiet, relaxing night in the country. The peace is interrupted by sounds. The sounds may be caused by animals — predators hunting prey. We feel safe inside our homes, away from the sounds.

Yet humans have a long history as part of nature. Alarming sounds still affect our instincts, sometimes making us nervous and edgy.

Throughout nature, animals use loud sounds to convey terror or aggression. They may be hunting their prey, fighting rivals for territories, repelling a predator, or trying to beat off competitors for mates.

The sounds can be fearsome, and they are often coupled with displays of size and strength. Sometimes an animal makes a warning noise. This is a relatively safe method of trying to scare an

Flashing lights are a visual warning. They are often accompanied by an auditory warning — the wail of a siren. If you cannot see one warning, you can usually hear the other.

DIY SCIENCE

THE WARNING RATTLE
Many people in rural areas of North and South America recognize the low rattle of the rattlesnake. It is a warning to let you know that if you come near, the snake may strike. Its bite can be deadly. The rattle at the end of the snake's tail is formed from large, hollow, cup-shaped scales. Mimic the rattle's clatter with this plastic version. A snake may have ten or more scales in its rattle, although they fall out with wear.

You need
Thin paper cups, brass fasteners, scissors.

1. Cut two pieces from the rim of a cup, as shown. Carefully make a small hole in each of the projecting parts and a set of small holes near the base, as shown.

2. Trim several cups in this way. Attach the rim holes of one cup to the base holes of the next cup with fasteners to form a chain. Shake the cups fast to rattle a warning to others.

SPECIAL FX

WAILING A WARNING
Burglar alarms, sirens, beepers, bells, bullhorns, speakers, and other devices are installed in many places. You can see them in banks, shops, offices, warehouses, factories, houses, vehicles, and even on people. During a walk, see how many of these you can spot. Sometimes they may sound because of a defect or a false alarm. When people get used to false alarms, they pay no attention to them — exactly the opposite of what is intended.

ANIMAL ALARMS

Here are some of the alarm and warning sounds made by wild creatures. The sounds may be a special version of the usual songs and calls made by the animal using its voice box. Or the sounds may be produced by actions, such as hitting or stamping. Often they are combined with visual displays for greater effect. Many types of animals respond to these sounds, so one warning works for many.

A snake hisses to show that it may strike.

When threatened by a predator, a toad hisses and puffs itself up to look bigger.

A frightened cat hisses, bares its teeth, and makes its fur stand on end to look bigger.

A gorilla shakes and rattles branches and may also beat its chest to chase away rivals and intruders.

Hisses are used as a warning by many types of animals, such as cats, snakes, toads, and some insects and spiders. People hiss to show suspicion or disapproval.

If a beaver sights a wolf or cougar, it slaps its tail on the water's surface in alarm.

A rabbit stamps its back legs hard to make a thump that travels through the ground.

Slap, thrash, rattle, and stamp — these sounds are made by an animal's actions, rather than by its voice box. The beaver's tail-slap travels well through the water to warn the rest of its family of danger.

An eagle preys from the air.

Ring-tailed lemurs live on the ground and in trees in Madagascar. If a lemur spots a predator flying overhead, it makes a certain alarm call, and the whole troop rushes to a hiding place on the ground. If the lemur sees a ground predator, it makes a different kind of alarm call, and the troop knows to climb trees to safety.

Warnings like these are especially common among woodland animals. They cannot see very far, or each other, through the layers of trees, twigs, and leaves, so warnings using sound are best.

enemy or threaten a rival from a distance. Once the situation escalates to physical contact and combat, the risks become far greater. Injuries are much more likely. In the wild, this often leads to death. If animals can settle disputes by sight and sound rather than actual fighting, they usually do.

The same kind of alarming sounds happen in modern towns and cities. The wail of a siren, an aggressive shout, and the cry of a frightened person are some of today's human equivalents to nature's warning sounds. The sounds make us alert, on edge, and ready for action.

These are some of the more unusual ways in which sounds have major effects on our minds and bodies. They alert and warn us of possible danger.

Sounds can have exactly the opposite effect, too — often in the

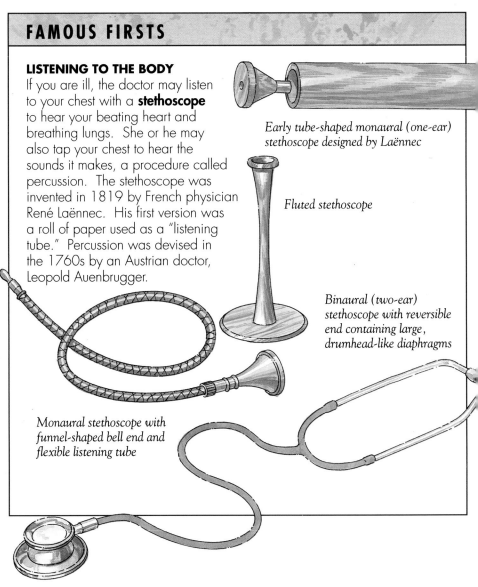

FAMOUS FIRSTS

LISTENING TO THE BODY
If you are ill, the doctor may listen to your chest with a **stethoscope** to hear your beating heart and breathing lungs. She or he may also tap your chest to hear the sounds it makes, a procedure called percussion. The stethoscope was invented in 1819 by French physician René Laënnec. His first version was a roll of paper used as a "listening tube." Percussion was devised in the 1760s by an Austrian doctor, Leopold Auenbrugger.

Early tube-shaped monaural (one-ear) stethoscope designed by Laënnec

Fluted stethoscope

Binaural (two-ear) stethoscope with reversible end containing large, drumhead-like diaphragms

Monaural stethoscope with funnel-shaped bell end and flexible listening tube

The heart can be scanned by ultrasound, using a technique called echocardiography. The resulting images are not as clear as other scanning techniques, such as CAT. But they have the advantage in that they are real-time or "live," and doctors can watch the heart actually beating.

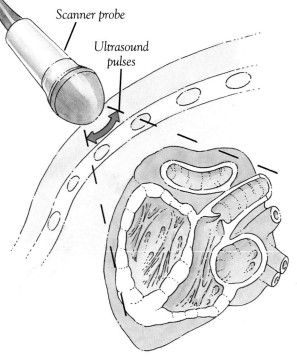

Scanner probe

Ultrasound pulses

The ultrasound scan is a method of producing a picture of the inside of the body. Ultrasonic sound waves, too high-pitched for humans to hear, are beamed into the body. Different parts such as bones, muscles, and blood vessels reflect the waves in different ways. The reflections or echoes are picked up and then processed by computer, and the resulting image is displayed on a screen. Many expectant mothers are scanned by ultrasound to check the baby's health. Ultrasound can also detect growths, tumors, and other abnormalities.

Ultrasound scan of a baby in the womb at 16-18 weeks.

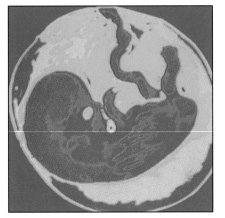

Echocardiogram of a living, beating heart. The main heart chambers are on the left.

DIY SCIENCE

HEAR YOUR HEARTBEAT

After Laënnec invented the first stethoscope, he advanced the paper roll to a wooden tube. One end of the tube was placed on the patient's chest, and the other to the doctor's ear. The modern stethoscope usually has a bell-end covered by a thin, flexible diaphragm, and hollow listening tubes leading to two ear pieces. But Laënnec's simple design still works well, as you can hear for yourself.

You need

Plastic funnel, plastic tube or hose, a cooperative patient, adult supervision.

1. To make a stethoscope, push one end of the plastic tube over the spout of the funnel to make a good seal.

2. Have an adult help you carefully place the stethoscope on your patient's chest.

3. With the hearing end to your ear, listen to the sounds. Place the funnel end on different parts of the chest. Can you hear the heart beating and the air whooshing in and out of the lungs?

FAMOUS FIRSTS

THE ECHO SOUNDS OF SONAR

Sound travels fast and far through water. Sonar — **SO**und **NA**vigation and **R**anging — uses sound to locate and identify underwater objects from fish to a submarine. Sonar works like radar but with sound waves instead of radio waves. Sound pulses bounce off objects. Hydrophones (underwater microphones) detect the echoes, and a computer analyzes the results. An early sonar system was developed by French scientist Paul Langevin in 1915 for ships to detect icebergs. It was greatly improved during World War I in order to detect enemy U-boats (submarines). Some types of sonar are called echo-sounders.

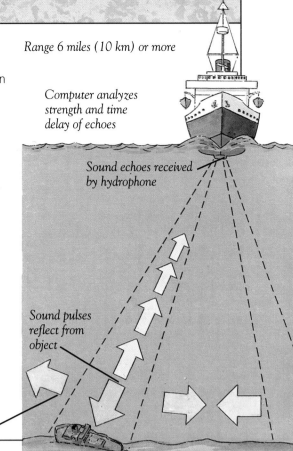

Range 6 miles (10 km) or more

Computer analyzes strength and time delay of echoes

Sound echoes received by hydrophone

Sound pulses reflect from object

Sonar pulses sweep back and forth across the seabed.

FASCINATING FACTS

- In the deep ocean, the sperm whale uses sound to hunt its prey. It sends out giant grunts, immensely powerful bursts of sound, that can disable nearby fish, squid, and other victims.

- In the middle of the night, people heard an eerie *tap-tap-tap* in an old building. They thought the noise was from a ghost or spirit, coming to take away the living, or returning with the souls of the dead. In fact, it was the deathwatch beetle, banging its jaws and head on wood, calling for a mate. The deathwatch beetle's grubs tunnel into oak trees and oak beams.

In a large choir, people are grouped according to the singing pitches of their voices. From high to low, and front to back, a simplified system of this is treble (boys and girls), soprano (high female), contralto (low female), alto (high male), tenor (medium male), baritone (deeper male), and bass (deepest male).

form of music. Musical instruments and styles of music can put us in different moods. A slow, soft song soothes and relaxes. A fast, loud one brings out energy and action in us.

A concert hall or dance club may contain masses of microphones and wires, arrays of switches and controls, and banks of loudspeakers. Yet many sounds are much simpler and just as pleasurable. We sing along with friends, cheer our heroes, and laugh and cry together. In every way, sound and its science is a vital part of our lives.

SPECIAL FX

SINGING SECRETS

Most people can carry a tune well enough. But excellent singing of classical and operatic music needs practice and training. One important technique is to sing from deep within the body. This means using the diaphragm and abdominal muscles to help the chest blow air from the lungs through the voice box. If you use the chest or neck muscles alone, the voice sounds tight, shallow, and strangled — and you soon run out of breath.

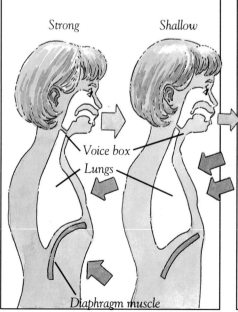

Strong   Shallow

Voice box

Lungs

Diaphragm muscle

SPECIAL FX

PAN'S PIPES

Pan was a Greek god of animals, known for his soothing music.

You need
Hollow bamboo or wooden tubes, tape, modeling clay, small saw, adult supervision.

1. Block off one end of a tube with clay. Place the other end to your lower lip and blow gently across the opening to make the pipe vibrate and create a sound.

2. Trim some tubes shorter for higher notes. Adjust the lengths until the tubes make a musical scale when blown one by one. Tape them in a row and play.

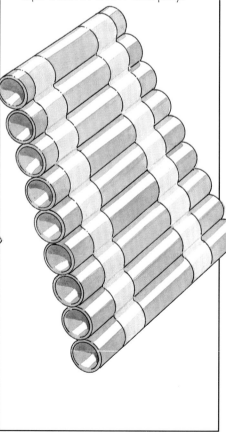

SPECIAL FX

SOUNDS MUSICAL

Most of us know when sounds are "music" rather than "noise." We can hear distinct sounds of certain pitches (frequency) that have a pleasing quality and blend well. In written music, each pitch, or note, is indicated on a set of five horizontal lines called a staff. The most common Western musical scale consists of sets of eight notes called octaves. The notes are written as duration symbols to indicate how long each pitch should sound. Other signs and words describe the speed, type of rhythm, loudness, and other features of the music.

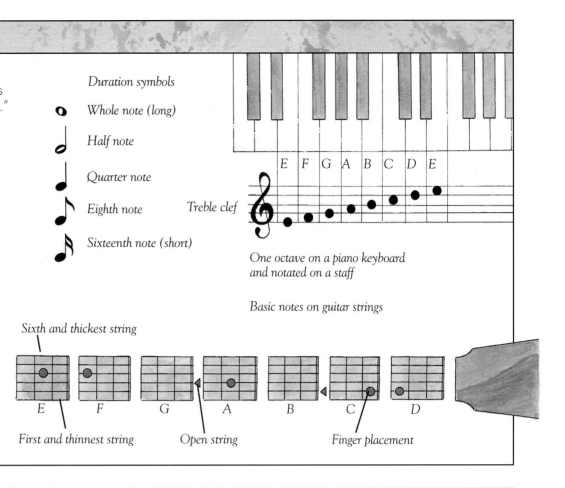

Duration symbols

𝅝 Whole note (long)

𝅗𝅥 Half note

♩ Quarter note

♪ Eighth note

𝅘𝅥𝅯 Sixteenth note (short)

Treble clef

E F G A B C D E

One octave on a piano keyboard and notated on a staff

Basic notes on guitar strings

Sixth and thickest string

E F G A B C D

First and thinnest string   Open string   Finger placement

FASCINATING FACTS

- Acoustics play a large part in the design of modern concert halls, theaters, and similar buildings. The journey of a sound wave can be shown on a computer screen for different frequencies and volumes of sound, for varying shapes of the hall's interior, and for different materials that are used. Many buildings have special disks, panels, and saucers on their ceilings and walls to absorb or reflect sounds.

- Huge cathedrals with their hard walls and floors of stone, glass, and wood are amazing places for acoustics. Almost any sound seems loud and long as it echoes and reverberates through the huge air space and bounces off the surfaces. This is why choirs in large churches sound so full and unique.

- In a recording studio, any stray sound is a nuisance. So the walls, ceilings, and floors are covered with sound-absorbing substances, such as wavy-surfaced tiles and thick carpeting. There is a continuing search for acoustically "dead" materials that absorb sounds.

The spectacular shapes above this concert stage add to the visual effect. But they are actually there to improve the auditory quality — to direct sound waves so the audience hears the music with the greatest clarity.

GLOSSARY

acoustics — a science that deals with the production, control, transmission, reception, and effects of sound.

amplification — the process of increasing or making greater.

atom — the smallest part of an element that can exist by itself or in combination with other atoms.

echo — a repeated sound caused by the reflection of sound waves.

echolocation — the navigational system of certain animals, such as bats and dolphins. The animals send out signals, called ultrasounds, that bounce or echo off the surroundings. The ultrasounds then return to the animal presenting a clear picture of its location and the objects in the area.

electromagnetism — a magnetic force developed by a current of electricity.

frequency — the number of vibrations per second of a sound wave.

infrasound — sounds too low for a human to hear.

kinetic energy — the force possessed by an object as it moves.

larynx — the upper area of the windpipe where the vocal cords are located.

molecule — the basic particle into which a substance can be divided and still be the same substance.

onomatopoeia — the process of inventing words that sound like sounds and using them in speech and writing.

pitch — the highness or lowness of a sound, especially a musical sound, that is determined by the frequency of the sound waves that are producing it.

resonance — a vital feature of acoustics wherein each object has a natural frequency of vibration depending on the object's size and shape, the thickness and flexibility of its material, how much air it encloses, and many other factors. When struck or shaken, the object vibrates at its natural resonant frequency, and so produces sound of a certain pitch.

sonagram — a diagram of sounds that shows the frequency and timing of the sounds.

sonar — a system that uses reflected sound waves to detect and locate objects.

stethoscope — a medical instrument that was developed to listen to sounds made in the body.

sympathetic resonance — resonance that occurs when it passes from one object to another.

triode — a valve that enlarges or amplifies electrical signals to make sounds louder electrically.

ultrasound — sounds too high for a human to hear.

wavelength — the distance between two similar points on successive waves.

WEB SITES

www.cinemedia.com.au/SFCV-RMIT-Annex/rnaughton/HERTZ-BIO.html

www.kids-space.org

www.edisonx.com/kids/

www.bio.bris.ac.uk/research/bats/ab_batpg.html

BOOKS

Animal Magic for Kids (series). *Bat Magic.*
    Dolphin Magic. (Gareth Stevens)

Exploring Our Senses (series). *Hearing.*
    Henry Arthur Pluckrose (Gareth Stevens)

Famous Lives (series). *Story of Alexander Graham
    Bell.* Margaret Davidson (Gareth Stevens)

Kids Can! (series). *The Kids' Science Book.*
    Robert Hirschfeld (Gareth Stevens)

Lasers: Humanity's Magic Light. Don Nardo
    (Lucent)

Lasers: The New Technology of Light.
    Charlene W. Billings (Facts on File)

Secrets of the Animal World (series). *Bats.
    Dolphins.* Isidro Sánchez (Gareth Stevens)

*Musical Instruments: From Flutes Carved of Bone,
    to Lutes, to Modern Electric Guitars.* (Scholastic)

Sign Language Made Simple. Edgar D. Lawrence
    (Gospel Publishing)

*Sign-Me-Fine: Experiencing American Sign
    Language.* Laura Greene and Eva B. Dicker
    (Gallaudet University Press)

Sound. Robert Friedhoffer (Watts)

Sound. Ron Marson (Tops Learning)

Sound and Music. Alan Ward (Watts)

Telecommunications: From Telegraphs to Modems.
    Christopher Lampton (Watts)

Telephones. Words Over Wires. Marcus Webb
    (Lucent)

Thomas Edison. Kelly C. Anderson (Lucent)

Thomas Edison - Alexander Graham Bell.
    Naunerie C. Farr (Pendulum)

VIDEOS

Dr. Dad: Sound - Radio Broadcasting. (GPN)

The Fabulous Five: Our Senses.
    (Rainbow Educational Media)

The First Moving Picture Show. (Phoenix/BFA)

The Five Senses. (Society for Visual Education)

Hearing and Sound. (Journal Films and Video)

How Does Sound Sound?
    (Coronet, the Multimedia Company)

How Does Sound Travel? (Encyclopædia
    Britannica Educational Corporation)

PLACES TO VISIT

Los Angeles Children's Museum
310 North Main Street
Los Angeles, CA 90012

Discovery Place
301 North Tryon Street
Charlotte, NC 28202

Discovery World
712 West Wells Street
Milwaukee, WI 53233

Science Center of British Columbia
1455 Quebec Street
Vancouver, British Columbia V6A 3Z7

INDEX